COUNTRY WALKS
AROUND BRISTOL

After a doctorate at Oxford University, Tim Mowl worked first as an Historic Buildings Inspector for the Department of the Environment and then as Architectural Adviser to the Bath Preservation Trust. His publications include the first study of the park gate lodge, *Trumpet at a Distant Gate* (1985), *Country Walks around Bath* (1986) and *John Wood: Architect of Obsession* (1988). He lives in Redland, Bristol.

Cover Illustration: Hawkesbury Church

COUNTRY WALKS AROUND BRISTOL

Tim Mowl

with illustrations by Alan Summers

Millstream Books

For Wendy

First Edition 1990

Millstream Books
7 Orange Grove
Bath BA1 1LP

This book is set in 9.75 on 11.25 point New Baskerville Type
by Ryburn Typesetting Ltd, Luddendenfoot, Halifax
Printed in Great Britain by BPCC Wheatons Ltd, Exeter

ISBN 0948975210

Contents

Introduction

What I shall remember about these Bristol walks are their changes of mood and their unpredictability. Three years ago I wrote *Country Walks around Bath* and there were some great circuits, but there was a sheltered, picture-postcard sameness about them. You know the scene – silver-haired retirees tending their dahlias in villages of mellow limestone nestled down deep in wooded valleys. In contrast the countryside around Bristol is wide open, it makes links, unexpected views keep opening up, its communities have changed and are changing.

How could I have predicted, when I went to explore the old collieries and brickworks near Pucklechurch, that they would be adrift with butterflies and blackberries? Or that there would be a brilliant group of gabled yeoman houses of the 17th century there, richer than anything the Cotswolds can turn up? Even prehistory is vibrant around Bristol and designed to communicate. That tremendous sequence of hillforts – Dolebury, Cadbury, Maes Knoll and Little Sodbury – make a chain commanding not only the area, but east to the Marlborough Downs and west across to Wales and King Arthur's Caerleon. I am still trying to work out why Dolebury is not nationally famous like Stonehenge. Go there and see what I mean. An Iron Age city with huge double ramparts of tumbled stone like something out of Tolkien, and all to yourself.

Then, of course, the tidal arms of the Severn snaking into the region are another part of its openness and variety. It is maritime without the sea. The church tower and sudden hummocks around Thornbury rising out of a white mist from the estuary are something I will not forget. Berkeley and Clevedon, both on the same Severn sea but so different, Oldbury another impact again. But I must not go on; down to business.

7

The walks are in three grades:

A	6–10 miles	Allow at least three hours, often more because there is so much to see, and take a refreshment break.
B	4–6 miles	A between meals walk. Try the Dundry one to get the feeling. It is nearer home and well-balanced.
C	2–4 miles	The merest stagger to get you going and remind you that you have legs. You will find the Hanham walk a revelation of hidden Bristol.

Though I am part of a two-car family I used a bus for almost every walk to see what I was letting people in for. Bristol coach and bus station in the early morning can be a chaotic tip and I grew to dread double-deckers that circumnavigate the housing estates of Yate, but I made it. Buses deserve support and if more people used them they would improve. All directions given assume a start from Bristol.

It is not possible to give rights of way a clean bill. Mr. Dickins and his helpers in the Avon County Council Planning Department have done an excellent job on stiles, but farmers can be single-minded. Cornfield and thorn barriers forced me to cut one walk near Pensford. Slurry from an overstocked farm did the same near Thornbury. Twice I had to avoid bulls and I found that a threatening stick helps with threatening dogs. So go wary.

One last point: could vicars get their act together, store valuables and let churches be open as they were built to be? At the moment some are, some are not; there is neither system nor reason and a church is, along with a pub, the welcoming place on a walk. We need them both.

Tim Mowl, Redland, March 1990

Publishers' Note

Maps. The maps for each walk are drawn to a scale of 1:30,000 (approximately 2 inches to 1 mile) except for Walks 1 and 7 at 1:40,000 (approximately 1.5 inches to 1 mile) and Walks 3 and 4 at 1:15,000 (approximately 4 inches to 1 mile). All significant features are included, whether necessary for establishing the line of the walk, or relevant for enhancing the enjoyment of the walk.

Rights of Way. All rights of way have been followed as far as possible according to the line shown on Ordnance Survey 1:25,000 Pathfinder maps. In some cases, where a right of way has been shown as crossing a field which is now ploughed or sown, the path has been altered to go round the edge of the field. All routes were checked in the spring of 1990, but if any path is subsequently found to meet such an obstacle, we suggest that you make your own detour, with reference to the appropriate Ordnance Survey Pathfinder map, always a useful adjunct to any walk. Walkers and farmers need to coexist amicably if our countryside is to be preserved, and it is only common courtesy for the walker to respect the work of the farmer.

Opening Times. The times given were correct in the spring of 1990, but are always liable to change in the future.

Buses. We have given the bus routes applicable in the spring of 1990. As routes and numbers may change, it is advisable to check with Badgerline Ltd before departure, and if you plan more than one walk in a week, you may benefit from various special fare offers. The telephone number for Badgerline in Bristol is (0272) 297979.

Under the Cotswold edge and back along the top of it – Old Sodbury to Hawkesbury

8.25 miles/Grade A

Maps: O.S. 1:25,000 Pathfinder ST 68/78
            O.S. 1:50,000 Landranger 172

Theme: An exhilarating walk, low and lush at first, then high and windswept all the way north, and then a spectacular change of landscape mood on the way back south. Easy underfoot with more lanes than footpaths.

Transport: By car – take the A432 out through Yate then turn left in Old Sodbury and park by the church (GR ST 756818).
By bus – not easy. A bus from Bristol coach station, such as the 628, will take you as far as *The Boot* at Chipping Sodbury. After that there are little red-and-white buses going on to Old Sodbury. Alternatively, walk on to the big roundabout, left up St John's Way, then immediately right into a cul-de-sac called Wickham Close. A footpath leads out of this between high walls and over a bridge. Thence a pleasant, reasonably well-stiled path over ten fields leads to Old Sodbury churchyard, but this adds three miles to the total if you repeat it on the way back.

Things to look out for:
1.   The hall where Tyndale translated the Bible
2.   An Art Nouveau tablet to a Californian Baron
3.   A stone bagpipes player
4.   A Norman manor with an early-Renaissance loggia
5.   A letterbox set in a Gothic window
6.   A Regency villa inhabited by a dog
7.   A prehistoric shippon

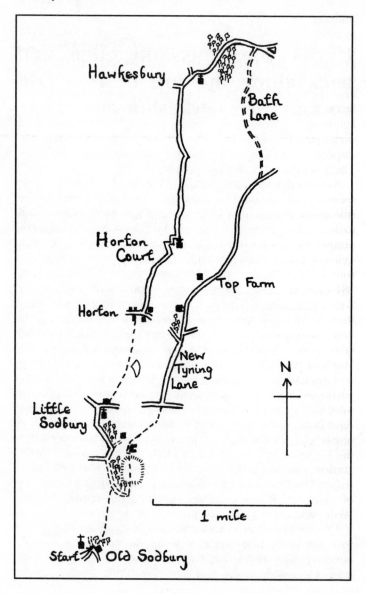

Itinerary

In most moods this is my favourite walk and if bits of it seem to poach on the Cotswold Way I was walking it long before that was thought of! From Old Sodbury church take the path alongside the school. It is marked by yellow arrows. Cross the fields, keeping near the hedge, and then a track brings you out onto the lane below Little Sodbury Manor. It has twice been struck by lightning, is said to have a badly-haunted bedroom and once sheltered William Tyndale. With an Iron Age fort next to it, one suspects continuous occupation over a phenomenal 3,000 years. The little church, St Adeline, is dull.

As the road forks to the right, march boldly through what seems like the backyard on the right of the cottage and take the stile over the fields, down below a reservoir, then steeply uphill to the road in Horton. Here a hefty infill has saved a particularly pretty Victorian school, not exactly muscular Gothic, but very well exercised. The lane below the school winds delightfully round Cotswold bastions. The tower on the hill was built in 1846 and commemorates General Lord Robert Somerset of Badminton. Horton Court and church are both so remarkable that all seven 'Things to look out for' could have come from here; and the church is kept religiously open. The Art Nouveau tablet is easy to spot, typically it looks to be made of plasticene. Much harder to locate is the bagpiper. There are two ostriches and two muzzled bears also in this rich building and the porch particularly proves by its decoration the theory that porches were socially more important than the church in the Middle Ages because that was where weddings were celebrated. This one is a beauty. Facing the chancel is a late Norman door into the Court, which dates back to 1150, and has a loggia in the garden built by a priest called William Knight who had visited Italy in Henry VIII's reign. Please don't just walk past this group of buildings. It deserves time and is open April—October, Wednesday and Saturday 2–6pm or by arrangement.

On past Upper Chalkley Farm with outstandingly drab barns to a stretch of lane overhung with nut bushes that literally bombard you in the autumn. Hawkesbury church is kept religiously shut which is a shame as the exterior is commanding.

The whole valley, ringed with woods and everything 16th century or earlier, has a poetic presence. The place is a veritable textbook of Cotswold stonework – at least four contrasted styles of masonry on the church walls and a perfectly graded slope of stone tiles on the barn across the road. This is where you should be looking out for a letterbox.

Turn up the hill into the dark wood, then, just on the outskirts of the rather ordinary village of Hawkesbury Upton, take the narrow track on the right, Bath Lane. It is at this point that the whole mood of the walk changes: no more architecture or cosy mediaeval villages, no more cow pastures. Instead there are great bare cornfields sown with stones and wide views over Wales and the Dean to your right, Badmintonshire and Wiltshire to your left. Try to plan for good weather because it is very exposed.

The first lane joins another one and after about two miles comes the first farm, Top Farm, on a lordly drive. At this point there are several modern houses and you can't help noticing that however well they manage the outline and the masonry they always spoil things with the windows by using prefabricated units. Then comes the fine Regency villa, all bow windows, that you must have noticed miles ago as you were walking up from that reservoir to Horton. It is a most elegant and un-Cotswold house, inhabited, so a notice on the gate tells you, by a fierce-looking Doberman Pinscher dog. I must say that he keeps the grounds perfectly mown and manicured.

Don't get lured downhill to Horton, but keep on high up along New Tyning Lane. As this reaches a T-junction go through the gap in the wall by the signpost and head straight across a ploughed field making for a stone stile. At the next ploughed field your marker is the bottom right-hand corner of the distant farmhouse. This is the home farm of the still almost invisible manor of Little Sodbury. If you walk along its lower range of oddly tarted up buildings you will find yourself facing the high ramparts of the Iron Age fort, before-mentioned. What is odd about it is that the two earth walls to the south are very widely spaced as if to form an enclosure for the cattle that they did not want messing up the central rectangle. The path

Norman doorway at Horton

cuts straight across the middle of the fort which, if you have done the Gordano and Churchill walks, you will find inferior to Cadbury and Dolebury. A stile leads to a steep downhill path through the wood where you will rejoin the field path to the left that was the first stage of your walk.

If you have the strength for another church before refreshment the one at Old Sodbury has a wooden effigy of a long-ago lord of Little Sodbury, otherwise its half-Norman, half-Gothic arcades have been scraped clean of interest. If you have not enjoyed this walk then you are due to emigrate.

Walk 2

On the trail of the mysterious prosperity of 17th century Pucklechurch

4 miles/Grade B

Maps: O.S. 1:25,000 Pathfinder ST 67/77
          O.S. 1:50,000 Landranger 172

Theme: Pucklechurch is no ordinary village. High, cool, grey and handsome, it has a quite unreasonable number of grand farmhouses that would be called halls anywhere else. They range from mid-17th century vernacular to early classical and this walk tries to present and explain them with a down-and-up loop over old miners' paths, abandoned rail tracks and pit banks overgrown with oak and bramble.

Transport: By car – take the B4465 out of Bristol through unfairly named Mangotsfield. Pucklechurch is only another three miles. Park near the church and the village centre (GR ST 699765).
By bus – the 389 from Bristol coach station will drop you at the *Fleur de Lys* pub. If you travel by car or bus, notice Dennisworth Farm on your left as you enter the village. It has eight gables and is a foretaste of what lies ahead.

Things to look out for:
1. Old enamel advertising plates on a real old-fashioned village grocers
2   A barley sugar pillared porch of 1678
3   All that is left of Brandy Bottom Pit
4   A nicely desolate brickworks
5   My candidate for the most beautiful unrestored house in Avon
6   An intact but gentrified colliers' village
7   Barns like castles
8   A wonderful central chimney stack

17

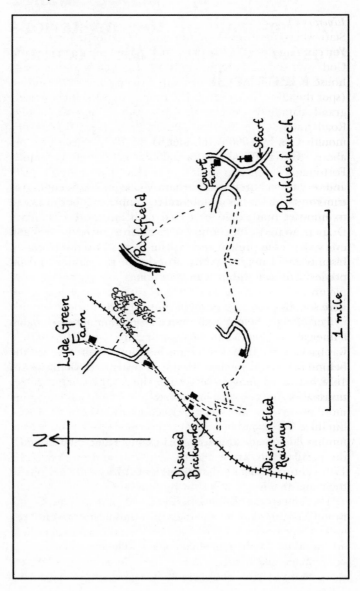

Itinerary

Start where Shortwood, Abson and Westerleigh roads meet. You can't miss it as the chapel actually says 'Prepare to meet thy God' over the door. Opposite is No. 1, an early 18th century house in crumbling grey lias with sixteen-pane sash windows (spot the fake casement). It is a preparation for the curiously grand scale of Pucklechurch living. Move along Westerleigh Road towards the church. Church Farm has 3-light ovolo-moulded mullions with the first of the high relieving arches above them. These are another Pucklechurch feature. Fortunately its glass front door is unique. The church is plain and very sharp-edged because hard limestone has been used to trim the softer lias. Sadly it is locked, so turn up Parkfield Road to enjoy 'C. Boulton & Sons, Grocers, Provision Merchants & Drapers' while it is still open. My favourite advert is 'Winalot, every dog's wheatmeal food' from the days when dogs ate biscuits and not tinned meat. Pucklechurch is into dogs and ponies. There is dung everywhere and lots of houses have pictures of their dogs on the doors with messages like 'I live here so watch out'; a friendly village.

Turn left up Kings Lane. Moat Farm behind the high wall is a fine gabled 17th century house but you'll see it better on the way back. As the lane bends right The Grey House tries to hide behind those dreary cypresses, but you can catch glimpses of its 1678 bulls-eyed gables, cross-mullioned windows and the very unusual twisted columns on the porch. Farming was becoming more prosperous with the introduction of clover in the 1650s, but these big, proud houses must have made their money from mining coal in the primitive bell pits that once pockmarked the parish. Only that explains their scale and number – the 17th century farmers of Pucklechurch ran small coal pits in their spare time.

The lane you are following is an old miners' path to the Brandy Bottom Pit. Miners were great on short cuts. They walked two abreast on a direct line between two points and there are rights of way in nearly every field. The lane becomes an occasionally muddy track. Climb the stile as the track bends sharp left and cross the huge sea of grass diagonally, taking

Bristol TV tower as a marker. Vast views of Wales and the Forest of Dean are opening up. Cross a stile in the left-hand hedge and turn right. When you reach the tarmac lane turn left until it peters out at a real, unrestored miner's cottage; then drive downhill steeply on the rough, watery path with blackberry bushes rioting and the wooded slopes of Brandy Bottom spoil heap on your left. The colliery was sunk about 1800, financed by Lord Radnor. It had two pits, one 205 yards deep and it closed in 1936. Winter is the best time for tracing the colliery yard and rail tracks because the vegetation is like a jungle in summer.

The path turns into a lane. At the grey farmhouse turn right to thread your way through the interesting wreck of Shortwood Brickworks. The 'Private' signs are only meant to keep you to the public way past the taller, square chimney, the desolate sheds and one still inhabited house.

Two short fields will bring you to a tempting lost railway track (Midland when it was working). But the path runs along the far side of the railway, not on it. Two fields and one farm (keep all the buildings on your right) will bring you back onto a lane. Turn left and ahead lies Lyde Green Farm. To me, its textures, gables, buttresses and old farm machinery are perfect. Some will want to restore it and inevitably that will be its fate. Savour it while it remains an honest working farm. It was built around 1651 in the Commonwealth about an earlier core. Visiting it, and the public path runs right in front of it, has taken you just a few yards out of your way. Retrace your steps to the lane and take the stile over into the pony-ridden field. Beware of a tame sheep that thinks it is a horse.

Two stiles take you over the abandoned railway again and the next stretch needs caution. Do not climb the hill but make diagonally across the field towards a wood at the end. You should hit another miners' track. this led to Parkfield Colliery, the one you see from the M4. It mined four veins of coal, one three feet thick, but by 1936 the coal face was five miles from the mine shaft. Water was a problem but not gas so the colliers could smoke as they worked. Don't be tempted far along the track to the right. As it quits the wood climb steeply up to the left until you reach a ruined stone building. Locals have

Lyde Green Farm

shamefully neglected this bit of the path and the gates are wrapped in barbed wire, but you can see the miners' way leading between the cottages. there are still the original fifty houses, all now interestingly tinkered with by their curiously isolated yet cheek-by-jowl residents.

Turn left along the houses to the end of the row. Here was once the colliery yard and inevitably there is, to the right, a very straight path heading across a giant field to Pucklechurch. It will bring you out at the *Rose and Crown* but there are still things to see. As you enter the village the towering barns and gables of Moat Farm are just viewable. At the church, turn left and look left to take in Pucklechurch House. With its severe Doric porch it represents the predictable classical tradition that was to elbow out the splendid vernacular work that we have been seeing. A little further along on the same side of the road lies Court Farm, the sixth and last 17th century pleasure of Pucklechurch. It stands confident and robust, topped with an amazing central stack, pre-1670, that carries six separate chimneys. Now, at least, as you loop back to the right to your car or bus, you know from personal experience the open breezy fields and pit-marked valleys that provided the wealth of wool and coal to fund such farmers' mansions.

A Quaker common and a wild, romantic valley – Frenchay and the Frome Gorge

3 miles/Grade C

Maps: O.S. 1:25,000 Pathfinder ST 67/77
            O.S. 1:50,000 Landranger 172

Theme: A walk that contrasts two improbable and incompatible survivals within the hidden arms of Bristol's northern suburbs – a village out of Mrs Gaskell with the demure houses of nonconformist gentry set around a green and, literally in their back gardens, a savage valley of thick woodland, loud water and ruined industry.

Transport: By car – make for Stapleton, just east of the M32, take the B4058 Frenchay Park Road, turn right into Begbrook Park Road before Frenchay Hospital and park on the common by the church with a spire (GR ST 638775).
By bus – Badgerline 628 from the coach station. Get off on Frenchay Common right by the carpark and church.

Things to look out for:
1   A quarrymens' village tactfully gentrified
2   Bootjack stiles
3   A picturesque turnpike cottage that nobody wants
4   A *retardataire* housing estate
5   The sources of all that Pennant stone which made Victorian Bristol
6   A refuge for suburban badgers

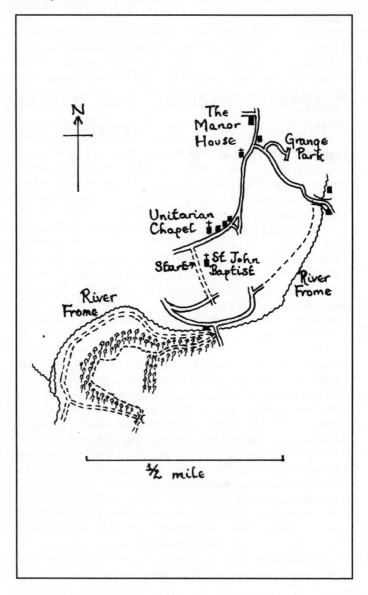

Itinerary

It is very West of England radical that St John Baptist, the Anglican church, should have been the relative newcomer (1843) in a village where Quaker and nonconformist chapels were already long established and intensely respectable. Indeed the ha-ha round the churchyard suggests that Rumley, who designed it, had been told to create a picturesque feature as well as a house of God. As you walk between the church and the village school you are crossing the divide between the well-spaced houses of the merchant gentry and the low-profile charm of the quarrymens' cottages. First turning on the right and pass the *White Lion* with its citified Edwardian scrollwork: too early in the walk to go in, but at least you know where it is in a notably un-pubbed area.

At Pearce's Hill turn left and plunge downhill into the improbable romanticism of the Frome gorge. Below you on the left, if you look over the wall, is some fancy Pennant stone edging on the path to Riverside Cottage, built for the manager of the Frenchay Iron Works. All around is the deep purple bloom of that Pennant stone which virtually created Redland and 19th century Clifton. The cottages are all Pennant and the cliffs they cling to are the wreck of Pennant quarries.

Turn right over the bridge across the Frome, a formidable little river when in spate and the power source for six or seven mills and foundries until the end of the 19th century. As you begin to climb the hill two paths branch off to the right. Take the uppermost of these through wooded quarries until you see a sign on the right marking a bridle path but little used as such. Follow this by its markers through the wood with the Frome rushing far below you. Cross the wide green field, keeping to the right-hand woodland edge until you reach a white notice warning horses, if they can read, to beware of pedestrians. An area of parkland path now slopes down by a small stream. Cross the rustic bridge and follow the path downhill. A feature of this strange area is the barely visible presence of vast housing estates on the edge of a mini-wilderness.

Down in the valley the Frome is enjoying a tranquil stretch with an island and clumps of bamboo. On the other side the

Begbrook trickles down a valley where badgers live almost in peoples' back gardens. Bear right and the rocks close in as the river rushes over two weirs with the arched relics of Frenchay Mill posed for a watercolour. Then abruptly you are back at the bridge again and the 'wild' loop of the walk is over.

Cross the bridge and turn right. The first weir upriver powered the Iron Works, but it will be sheer quarry faces to the left and the cottages which served it that grab your attention. Turn right along Chapel Lane. The Wesleyan Chapel has suffered a conversion, but you might notice the pollarded hornbeam hedge climbing the hill behind it.

Follow the path (the moistest bit of this walk) along the river to Cleeve Wood Bridge – an unusually massive structure to carry a minor road and an instance of how seriously the turnpike trusts took their duties and investments. The 1823 iron marker is set halfway across the bridge and, though we are not going that way, it is worth crossing to see the 1798 iron mill down by the river on the left, and the inexplicably deserted turnpike cottage on the right. Why this charming Italianate structure set among flowering trees and overlooking National Trust land ten minutes from the city centre should be abandoned is a mystery.

Back across the bridge and up the road between beetling miniature cliffs brings us to Grange Park, a 1950s housing estate that defied the architectural fashions of its day. When English house-building was uniformly drab and utilitarian some eccentric developer insisted that Grange Park should go up in a boxy Cotswold vernacular with Gothic dripstones over almost every window. For its date it is a prodigy, but it is oddly sullen in aspect. Across the road is the village hall by Sir George Oatley who designed the University Tower at the top of Park Street. Here he was wearing his Arts and Crafts hat.

Back now on the common and Beckspool Road we are in Frenchay's gentry belt with a quite outstanding sequence of 18th century façades behind high garden walls and fences. Another diversion, but a very short one to the right, is needed to see The Manor House – a Bath stone interloper in a Pennant and stucco district. Almost certainly the work of John

Frenchay Unitarian Chapel

Wood's rival John Strahan, the architect of Redland Court, it is an impressive but overactive design crowded with weak detail and is only one room thick. Strahan stuck the single storey wings onto the main house to give it at least two stylish entertainment rooms. This absent-minded design must have impressed later residents of Frenchay because several other large houses, like Fromeshaw House across the road, have imitated it. As you retrace your steps back to the village hall you will notice one of the smallest lodges in Britain growing out of the high wall on your left.

Now comes the architectural high point of the walk – a series of highly individual Georgian merchant houses with the two chapels that served their exacting spiritual needs. Interestingly, the Wesleyan Chapel of the quarrymen down the hill has closed shop, but these two élite establishments on the common, the first a plain, satisfying Quaker rebuild of 1809 and the second a Unitarian Chapel, survived as going concerns. The Unitarian Chapel was first built at the end of the Commonwealth. If you are lucky enough to be let in, it has an inner 'Crinoline' door, if not you can still enjoy the weathercock which represents Halley's comet on either its 1759 or 1835 visitation.

Cedar Hall is another of these low-winged houses with a heavy neo-Georgian infill, then come Frenchay House, Clarendon Lodge and Clarendon House; this last looking with its ironwork like a stray from Cheltenham. The Old House next door has a dour façade of about 1780 added to an older structure and across the road are a pair of 1795 houses built with paired coach houses as a speculation by a Dr Bradford. They would be more at home on Kingsdown and look like a Thomas Paty design, but they add a note of authority to the common. The one nearest the church was for many years the rectory. And that, with a reminder of the *White Lion* just round the corner, brings us back to the starting point.

A Hunting-Town walk – Berkeley and Ham

Just under 2 miles/Grade C, but teeming with things to see

Maps: O.S. 1:25,000 Pathfinder ST 69/79
          O.S. 1:50,000 Landranger 162

Theme: For my town walks I like atmospheric places, delicately run-down with the undisturbed textures of the centuries. Berkeley is perfect: half Holland of the marshy estuary and 18th century trade, half a hunting-town of the 19th century gentry. Take your time over this brief walk to savour the curious mood of streets and lanes.

Transport: By car – the A38 north from Bristol is itself something of a ghost road since the M5 opened. It has empty dual carriageways and vacant-looking motels waiting for a Hitchcock. Turn left on the B4066 and park near the prominent Town Hall – 1810-ish Bath stone ashlar (GR ST 684993).
By bus – in perfect preparation for the pace of Berkeley life, the very slow 306 from Bristol coach station to Gloucester will drop you off in Salter Street by the Town Hall.

Things to look out for:
1   Traces of a lost port
2   A sea mill with no water
3   A Norman deer park
4   Horses as beautiful as any in a Stubbs painting
5   The real patterned gloom of the Middle Ages
6   By-products of a Bristol brass founding
7   Stable backs

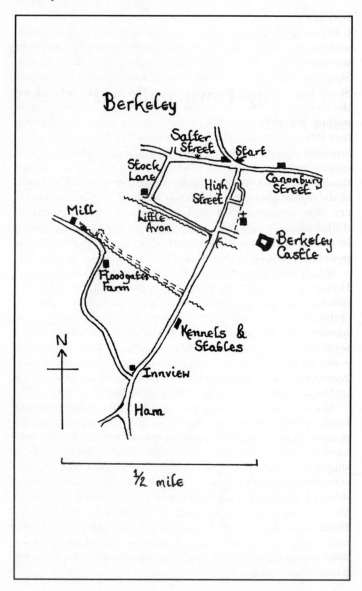

Berkeley

Salter Street

Start

Stock Lane

High Street

Canonbury Street

Mill

Little Avon

Berkeley Castle

Floodgates Farm

Kennels & Stables

N

Innview

Ham

½ mile

Itinerary

If Berkeley's four main streets represent, as some say, a Roman settlement, then the Romans here employed drunken surveyors, but it helps to know the names. West from Market Square is Salter Street, south is High Street, east is Canonbury Street and north is Marybrook Street. Be alert all the time for the contrast between the relaxed mellow brick of 18th century trading prosperity and the much harsher brick and outlines that followed in the 19th century when fox hunting became a favoured display of gentry money and Berkeley Hunt with its canary yellow colours was mildly fashionable. The exciting thing about this walk, even if you believe foxes should be gassed or die of lead poisoning, is that you can hear that belling hound cry that Shakespeare found so poetical (see Theseus in *A Midsummer Night's Dream*) and watch horses pop neighbourly heads out of Gothick stable doors. In Berkeley only the nuclear power station is dead. The 19th century still lives.

Set off west along Salter Street. No. 9 on your left and Salter House on your right are perfect illustrations of the difference between the way Georgian and Regency handled classical architecture. The first is crowded and tense with windows; the second is cool and laid back with space all around its five windows. You will begin to notice a curious feature of this town – the number of wide doors apparently for very fat people! Numbers 21 and 23 on your left actually share a porch to keep up the fat effect but the modern door to No. 23 is unhappy.

At the *Mariners Arms*, significant name, turn left down Stock Lane. At the bottom on the right, Berkeley's 18th century prosperity is marked by the big, dreaming house with cambered windows and patterned brick. Below it is a supportive row of small houses that once lined a quay. All that remains of water as you turn left along Jumpers Lane is a deep ditch of the divided Little Avon river. This brims with water flora – purple loosestrife, water forget-me-nots, comfrey and Himalayan balsam among the reeds. A hundred years ago the coal and salt trows moored here and the corner house at the main road still has the low wooden door through which salt was passed into the cellars.

31

Turn right over the bridge. There is an evocative glimpse of the castle upstream and an even better one if you deviate onto the footpath to the left. Both the castle and the nuclear power station, clearly visible on your right, have low menacing profiles, oddly evil in their contrasted impressions of power.

A short walk along the road leads to a right-hand turn up a rough lane. A lifebuoy stands prepared for rescue from water all of two feet deep. As the lane crosses the stream back onto a tarmac road it is worth a short detour right to see the sea mill. First on the right is the bland mill owner's house, 1750 like the mill, but brick where the mill is crumbling sandstone. A tidal stream once worked the mill's machinery, then steam power from the brick chimney. It still grinds flour.

Turn back down the lane past Floodgates Farm, a double-pile house whose straight-topped windows suggest a date of a decade or two later than the cambered-headed windows of the mill owner. The lane winds into Ham, an estate village inset with Berkeley coronets (the last Earl died in 1942 but the family survives in the castle). With luck the 'music' of the hounds should be loud here and it is worth a pause before you turn back left towards the town. To the right are the harsh dark houses of the 19th century set around a green. Beyond, rises the hill of the deer park which is still thronged with fallow deer. Immediately on your left, Innview cottage shows what rural life was like before the big 19th century rebuildings. Its side wall has the profile of an early 17th century one-storeyed stone building. This was heightened with brick in the 18th century. In living memory a man lived here with 14 children and kept himself on the produce of his vegetable garden. The children slept in the attic, marked now by a blocked window.

A short walk past the fine early 19th century Gothick house on the right are the Kennels and Stables of the same date and style. All the howling noises have been coming from here and the horses are usually as curious to see you as you are to see them. It is a gate to linger over.

The straight road back between the two bridges is a brief repeat of the outward journey. On the right a private way to the castle goes under a little gate house that was brought here in the

Mill chimney near Berkeley

1920s from Yate Court. If you visit the castle later watch out! The best two rooms in it were contrived to look mediaeval in the same 1920s period. St Mary's Church, easily reached from this little road, is, like Berkeley town, more interesting and atmospheric than actually beautiful. It has preserved the all-over patterning and gloom so common to the 13th century and it is kept open and welcoming. The tower is of 1753, Georgian Gothick and not quite what it seems.

With the High Street some serious house-spotting can begin. Numbers 58 and 56 retain early 18th century cross-mullions and their brick walls rest on stone foundations. But No. 42 rests on virtually eternal blocks of black slag from the Bristol brass foundries. All along this street are wide entrance doors to rear stables where hunters' horses were boarded out in the season. After No. 36 a mania for bow windows sets in. Spot the recent fakes by their rough brickwork and wide mortar joints. The antique shop sector has good 19th century shop fronts. Up Church Lane is the old Vicarage – early 18th century with a hipped roof and pineappled gate piers. Dr Jenner's hut in its garden is a charming 18th century root house that can be visited from April to October. Then the Halifax office on the corner of Market Place has the date 1666 in pargetting over the porch.

Only Canonbury Street to the right really deserves further exploration and it leads conveniently to the castle. On your way there spot more brass slag foundations to the *Berkeley Arms*. Across the road in Ruskinian Gothic with trails of ivy and oak is the Police Station and Petty Sessional Court. After this and the blocked-up forge, Berkeley peters out in green fields, gloriously un-suburbed and rural. Such a short walk can have given you no excuse for tiredness, but I have always wanted to spend what must be a very Betjemanesque night in the *Berkeley Arms*. Perhaps someone more confidently idle than I might give it a try.

Walk 5

Severnside warths – the dyke lands and tumps of Oldbury and Littleton

7.5 miles/Grade A (but easy)

Maps: O.S. 1:25,000 Pathfinder ST 49/59 & ST 69/79
          O.S. 1:50,000 Landranger 172

Theme: An unusual, quirky countryside of dim villages and deep-cut streams, intensely estuarine in feeling and gusty with winds that rush in over mud flats. This is a cheerful walk to blow the cobwebs away and, though the sudden hillocks make it anything but flat, it is not a strenuous Grade A.

Transport: By car – north on the old A38 ghost road through Almondsbury, then left into Thornbury on the B4061. Make for the high tower on the north-west of the town and park near the church (GR ST 634906).
By bus – the regular service 310 from Bristol coach station winds endlessly round Thornbury's new estates but eventually puts you down quite close to the church. But if you get off at the bus station a walk down the long main street will give you an interesting foretaste of the homely local building style. Perversely, I suppose, I get more satisfaction out of the confident 19th century Italianate Nat-West bank, but The Chantry on your right has a lively 18th century Gothick doorway.

Things to look out for:
1   Probably the earliest formal garden building in Britain
2   The half-built palace of the man who should have worn Henry VIII's crown
3   Topiary work to shame Henry Moore
4   A village of front bridges as well as front doors
5   A feminist saint who chose death not dishonour
6   Sluice gates on the warth
7   A local liking for two attic storeys

35

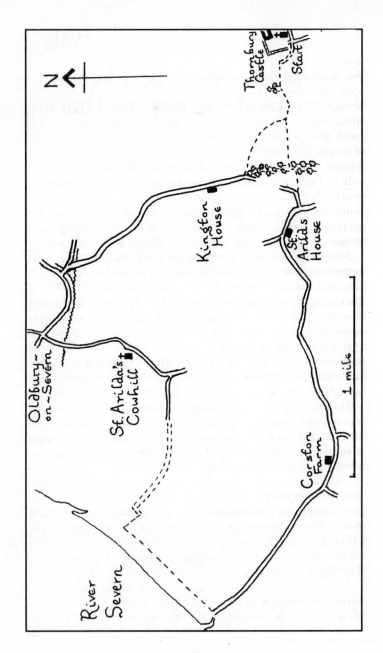

Itinerary

You might look into the church, if only because it is usually open, but after the south door, which hesitates interestingly between Norman and Early English Gothic, the high, ambitious interior is dull. Look out for the Stafford knot in the south aisle chapel. Round the back of the churchyard is a wall of empty bay windows overlooking the graves. This was built around 1511 and the theory is that it was meant as a galleried walk to look down on the formal knot gardens of the interior court. Thornbury was always more a palace than a castle so it could have this sophisticated feature, but why the bay windows overlooking the church? The castle is now a very pricey hotel so save it for your return if you are in that league; I'm not.

Now take the rough lane that dives off downhill to the left immediately before the castle lodge. Looking back you get pleasantly tousled views of the castle. The great Duke of Buckingham, who was executed before he finished it, must have been an enthusiast for hawking because the marshes came right up to the castle walls in the 16th century. Its towers were for show not defence. The Duke had also obtained royal licence to found a college with dean, sub-dean, eight priests, four clerks and eight choristers, but his disgrace and execution brought this design to an end.

Fork left on the track signposted to Kington and follow it across a huge field of red earth to the farm on a lane. Here you turn right for Oldbury, passing Kington House on the way with its show of abstract sculpture clipped out of yew trees. After the bridge turn left into the village.

Oldbury is an odd place. It has a sub-maritime air with the unreasonably deep stream bed on your left crossed by bridge after bridge to the cottages on the other side. Tides are obviously a feature and so are commuters. Almost every house has one of those massive iron name plates that new arrivals in the country like to buy to announce 'Honeysuckle Cottage' or 'The Moorings'.

At the T-junction there is a choice of inns. The *Ship* and the *Anchor* are reminders of the old eel and salmon fisheries. Turn left over the river past the *Anchor* and up the hill to St Arilda's, high on its tump. Walkers can get blasé about views but the scene from the north porch of this church is something special, with the Severn Bridge dramatising an already dynamic composition of estuary water and Forest of Dean hills. I have, however, been here on a day of dense fog when I had the eerie experience of hearing the Berkeley Hunt pass through the fields nearby without being able to see a single horse or hound. The present day church occupies the site of a former Roman camp and its tower used to carry a spire. This was blown down in 1703. 'Saynt Arild Virgin', by the way, was 'martired at Kineton ny Thornberye by one Muncius a tiraunt, who cut off hir heade becawse she would not consent to lye with him'.

Continue down the road to Cowhill and turn right up a dead-end lane. I have tried to keep to tarmac on this walk because the local mud can be lethal in wet weather. The lane meanders past some 18th century farms getting steadily more reed and ditch surrounded, turning into a track, then into a path ending up on the warth or dyke. This runs high and reasonably dry between the low fields and the exhilarating sweep of Severn sand and water. Turn left along it and enjoy the sheer un-Englishness of the scene for a mile until you come to a battery of sinister iron sluice gates that seem to go to a lot of trouble to control a trickle of water. A good road comes right up to the warth here to serve an unexpected factory. Take it into Littleton where the marshes end and lively miniature hills begin. Keep straight on uphill ignoring two right turns but stopping to give Corston Farm its due.

This is a strikingly tall 17th century building which is being sensitively restored. It has the first of the two-storeyed gables which, rather like elvers and St Arilda, are a local speciality. The lane winds up and down Titters Hill to St Arilds House, a fairly stark late-18th century farmhouse which makes a point of totally disregarding the local vernacular style. Turn right here and just around the next corner you will see some more two-storey gables at Willow Farm. Before you reach Fewsters Farm, which has three gables facing you but no less than five on the other side, turn left and take the first gate on your right. This opens into a track leading through a narrow belt of woodland

St Arilda's church, Cowhill

to join your original route out from Thornbury Castle where that expensive gourmet dinner you probably haven't booked is waiting for you.

Bristol's personal limestone wilderness in a devious circuit around Ashton Court

4.5 miles/Grade B

Maps: O.S. 1:25,000 Pathfinder ST 47/57
           O.S. 1:50,000 Landranger 172

Theme: The suburban sublime, no less; an outstanding circuit hard to match on the edge of any major city. An 18th century landscaped park, mature woodland, an early classical mansion and then the towpath into the Avon Gorge with Clifton across the river like a Georgian Tibet and the Suspension Bridge slung airily above. After that, Nightingale Valley and an Edwardian set of villas is almost an anticlimax.

Transport: By car – to the Clifton Suspension Bridge on the B3129 out of Clifton. Cross the bridge (15p toll) and park in the third road on your right, Church Road near the church, then walk back to the B3129 and you will see the starting point – the big lodge to Ashton Park towering ahead of you across the main A369 road (GR ST 558727).
By bus – the 358 to Portishead from Bristol coach station will put you down at Ashton Park Lodge.

Things to look out for:
1   18th century dew-ponds for deer
2   The grandest council house in Bristol
3   All that's left of a lost railway station
4   Samuel Plimsoll's bust
5   The foot of a Victorian funicular railway
6   Surrey in Bristol

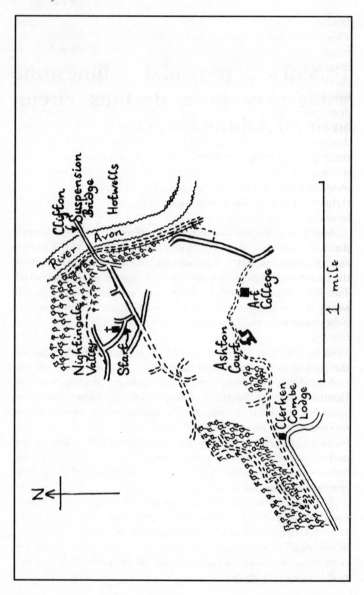

Itinerary

This first lodge is impressive but late, about 1880; there is a much more romantic one ahead – the Smyths of Ashton Court housed their estate workers in style. Follow the drive, with its carefully arranged glimpses of the city between small woods below you, then take the second drive up to the right by the first deer pond away from the walled garden. A broad meadow between two woods will open up to your left sloping gently downwards. Keep close to the left-hand line of wood until you come to a large block of fallen tree trunk. There is a gap here in the fence with no gate, only posts. Go through it and you will immediately join the Nature Trail at a post marked NT4. Turn right and follow it; the rusty iron fencing was the 18th century boundary to the deer park.

At first the wood is rather bare of flowers, but in summer there are lots of brown wood butterflies. Fork left at NT10 and zig-zag down Pill Grove, then at the bottom turn left, not on the broad track but on the narrower path nearest the park wall. This bit is muddy in wet weather. The second round pond is worth a pause if only for the brilliant range of dragonflies hovering above it. They are becoming quite rare as ponds get filled in. This one was built of squared Pennant stone blocks in 1765 by Sir John Hugh Smyth. There is no running stream in the park so it was a practical necessity.

Now the wonderfully textured and romantic Clerken Combe Lodge, designed in 1810 by Henry Wood, opens up against the wooded hillside. It looks much more like a mediaeval monastery gateway than most real ones do. The lucky council tenants who live in it use both sides of the archway. The room over the arch was used by the last of the Smyths as a *maison de plaisance* where she watched birds with her chauffeur.

Follow the drive down into the park. Stinking hellebore, not everyone's taste in flowers but handsome, bloom here in winter. On the left is a high deer fence and a whole herd of fallow deer to enjoy. Turn right at the T-junction by the big copper beeches and watch out for cars on this drive as you make towards Ashton Court.

The house is confusing approached from this angle, but you can usually buy an ice-cream at this point as you sort things out. The right-hand wing of the house which you can see end-on was one of the earliest and most ambitious (I didn't say beautiful) classical buildings in Britain when MP Thomas Smyth built it in 1632–3. Inigo Jones certainly did not design it; the rhythm of its windows is far too halting. Almost everything else that you see from this side is a late-Georgian muddle by the same Smyth who made the deer ponds. It is worth peering through the big bow window on the left to see the sad wreck of the Gothick library. All the bits are still there but there is no money to put them together again. Polltax payers please note!

Unless you are going for a meal in the restaurant, take the drive that swings up above the house. Below is the stable range where the Lord Mayor's coach is kept. The house and park were bought by Bristol Corporation in a stroke of inspired good sense in 1959.

Now the drive drops steeply downhill past a bottled oak tree. The tower block on your right houses the polytechnic's Faculty of Art and Design but the only positive comment to make on its design is that the tall trees almost hide it. The students' art exhibitions are well worth a visit, often livelier and cheaper than professional shows.

At the main road you come to the one brief traffic-smashed part of the walk, so cross the road, turn left along Bedminster cricket ground and get it over quickly. At the end of the ground turn right up the narrow path that then runs alongside the railway line to Portishead. If you are lucky there will be splendid police horses in the paddock on the left, but if your luck is out you will only see a grey donkey. Cross the line on the very rickety bridge which served the platforms of the old Clifton Bridge station and take the left-hand path towards the Gorge.

Now comes the sublime section and that is no exaggeration. Across the Avon all the terraces of Clifton swoop up with a surprising amount of native woodland surviving between them. The muddy foreshore has a rich marine flora but it is treacherous underfoot. Walk on between the river and the railway, noting, if you can keep your eyes off the Suspension

44

The remains of Clifton Bridge Station

Bridge, the old mooring bollards at regular intervals. It was never easy to get sailing boats up this stretch of the Avon. Under the bridge, Hotwells and the lost cliff railway are across the water, but it is no use looking for the hot well, it was always below the high tide mark and the spa room was smashed when they built the noisy Portway. Have you spotted Plimsoll yet?

At the first railway bridge, turn left and climb up Nightingale Valley. There is a rich flora on this limestone with rare whitebeam bushes. Stokeleigh Camp, an Iron Age fort, is high above you on your right. Few cities have a picturesque wilderness like this so close in. Bear left a little when you reach the road and then right along Church Road. The highly desirable houses of this suburb are oddly alien to Bristol – mostly brick, tile and timber, all turreted, towered and gazeboed to take in the views. The church has an Arts and Crafts top to a High Victorian bottom and the lychgate seems made for a Merchant-Ivory film of an E.M. Forster novel but 'No Dogs Please'. By the bold Italianate Towerhurst you have probably left your car, or the bus-stop is just across the way. Match this for a suburban walk if you can!

Two castles and the Gordano

8.5 miles/Grade A

Maps: O.S. 1:25,000 Pathfinder ST 47/57
       O.S. 1:50,000 Landranger 172

Theme: The Gordano, a marsh between two limestone hills and the most intensely individual area of Bristol's hinterland. It has been half-wrecked, half-dramatised by the cutting of the motorway, and this walk shifts wildly from scenic sublime to scenic vandalism, wild wood, wide vistas, history and havoc.

Transport: By car – drive to Clevedon and park as near the pier as possible (GR ST 402718). If you feel lazy, drive up the coast road north and park by Walton St Mary church. That will save you a climb at the start but give you another at the end.
By bus – Bristol to Clevedon X7 is the most direct and get off near the pier.

Things to look out for:

1	Castle View – Clevedon's distinctive Gothic
2	The last real castle or the first fake fortress?
3	A Gothick gazebo
4	A weedy vineyard
5	Rhines
6	The prehistoric Anglo-Welsh connection
7	A whole wood of whitebeam
8	A bridge horsewomen are not supposed to ride over

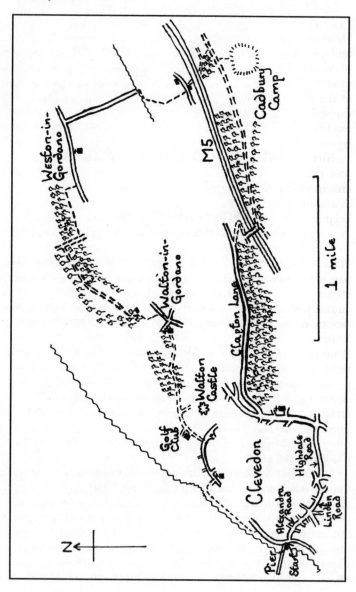

Itinerary

Head north past the entrance to Clevedon's reconstructed pier and turn left at the first church down the cliff path. The views of Wales are exhilarating yet have the desolate Severnside muddy quality. Where green lawns sweep down, climb back up to the road and a spiky church where lazy motorists can join the walk. The road uphill is lined with Victorian villas, the essential Clevedon of Bristol retirees. Castle View on the right is outstanding for its bay windows.

Turn up to the Golf Club on the left and follow the track past the club house. If you look back right, Walton Castle crowns the hill. Lord Paullett built this oddity in James I's reign as a hunting lodge with defensive undertones. It has a central keep for noisy revels and a circle of motel-type towers for discreet dalliance. There is nothing else quite like it in Britain.

Now the Gordano is opening up and the dim throb of the M5 is already echoing from its new cliffs. The track leads down past the greens, a wood, a field and a second wood. Up to the left is a Gothick garden house in one of those private landscapes that make England so attractive and infuriating. It deserves repair. Walton-in-Gordano church is an ugly little brute, mostly 1838 but at least it is unlocked. The village, like Weston-in-Gordano, is a trifle stony and hard-faced. Cut down right to the main road then left to the edge of the village where a stile on the left leads you up into the woods and marjoram slopes of the common. Here the tracks are confusing but if you make diagonally across, both north and to the seaward slope, uphill all the way, you'll find a broad track through a dark pheasant-infested wood. When this leads to a T-junction, strike downhill to the right.

At the wood's end, bear left along the edge of the wood to the second field which is a large, east facing vineyard. Follow this round down to the lane and turn left for Weston-in-Gordano which has a pub, the *White Hart*. It is perhaps a little too early for refreshment so borrow the key to the church instead. Its choir stalls have two crude peacock misericords and the vestry has an elegant bust of Spencer Perceval, the assassinated Prime Minister, who came from a local family.

Now steel yourself for the rowdy bit. In the village, take the first right turn after the pub and cross the Moor. This is like a lost scrap of the famous Somerset wetlands with deep rhines draining the land. After crossing the widest rhine a series of gates leads you diagonally right across the fields on the vaguely marked path to the lane. All this time the M5 racket will get worse. Be brave, turn left at the lane, then right immediately after Wynhol Farm. A stony bridlepath leads steeply uphill under the concrete viaduct, passing homes of people who must have thought they were retreating to the peace of the countryside! At the top of the hill, turn right along Cadbury Camp Lane until you see the stile and National Trust marker on the left. This is Cadbury Camp and it certainly merits a detour. In any decent weather the views are staggering – Wales from the Black Mountains to Barry, then Steep Holm, the whole sweep of the Quantocks and round over Mendip right into Wiltshire. Only the northern aspect is brief. If King Arthur did not use this Iron Age fort then he had no eye for communication. The double defensive ditches are still 20 feet deep, full of flowers and preserving much of the original stone screes.

Back on Cadbury Camp Lane heading west you plunge into the rarest of British wood, one with a high proportion of whitebeam trees and richly berried limestone exotica. The sandy lime is popular with young men jogging with their exhausted dogs and the peace from the hidden motorway is striking.

Then, suddenly, Wagnerian drama! A right turn and you are on the edge of an echoing cacophonous canyon of cars. Now you know what that crazy, high spiderweb of concrete, slung over you as you drove the M5, was built to carry – you and a few horses. But according to the notice horseriders must dismount to cross the gulf, and two mounting blocks have been provided. All I can say is that the 14 year old girl who was riding over when I was there sat firmly on her pony's back.

Equally abruptly on the other side the noise is lost. You turn sharp right down into the wood to Clapton Lane and walk left past disused quarry entrances into Clevedon. If you were one of those who parked up at Walton St Mary keep your eyes open for a narrow path to the right by No. 2 Conygar Close. This will

50

A Gordano rhine

take you between the suburban houses to the Walton road. Turn right, then left uphill and you will be sweating your way back to the golf course turn where it all started. Other walkers merely continue into Clevedon enjoying the deeply Victorian All Saints church with its even better vicarage on the bosky slopes beyond. Living in Clevedon must be an oddly sheltered experience and an acquired taste as the town is more time-trip than holiday resort.

Walk 8

Three wild forest combes and a pastoral contrast – Cleeve, Backwell and Brockley

8 miles/Grade A, and it will take longer than you think

Maps: O.S. 1:25,000 Pathfinder ST 46/56
          O.S. 1:50,000 Landranger 172

Theme: Contrast – trees so close overhead that they hide the sun, a forest tract where it really might help to take a compass, a frightening gash in the earth, then pastoral calm unchanged in the last two centuries – a long but exhilarating walk.

Transport: By car – take the A370 south out of Bristol heading for Weston-super-Mare and park in Cleeve near the *Lord Nelson* (GR ST 457657).
By bus – the 351 or 352 for Weston from Bristol coach station. Get off at the *Lord Nelson* in Cleeve.

Things to look out for:
1   Dramatic darkness at noon
2   Downland flora and fauna
3   The home of a mediaeval warren master
4   A maze of conifers
5   The setting for a thriller film finale
6   A tower too sophisticated to be quite credible
7   A chocolate box cottage orné
8   The Pirate's Grave

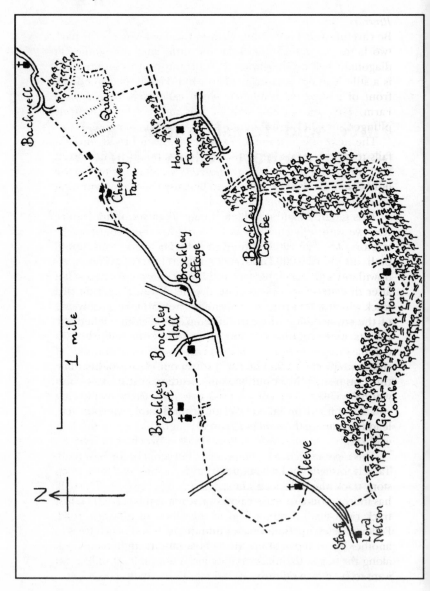

Itinerary

Be careful over this first bit. Next to the *Lord Nelson*'s car park two lanes enter together. Take the little lane that comes in diagonally behind the garage. A short way up this on the right is a stile leading across a field to white kissing gates and the front of a superior residence which calls itself Walnut Tree Farm. Hug the garden wall of this and you are abruptly plunged into an English jungle – this is Goblin Combe.

The next mile is quite an experience. Even bright sunlight fails to penetrate as the path leads up between high walls of rock almost hidden by straight-boled trees all reaching for the light. Even the yews grow tall, and because there is no running water the silence seems unnatural.

This gloomy idyll is broken by the Goblin Combe Nature Reserve with ugly conifers and the muddy track shattered by tractors. At a Nature Reserve sign take the steep, stony, uphill path on the left through nut and birch scrub. The open downland with views, flowers and butterflies comes as a relief after the claustrophobic combe. A gate and stile open onto a track which soon brings you to the Warren House – surely one of the most isolated houses in Avon. Once it controlled the rabbits of Wrington Warren. Now comes the bit where a compass might help though I managed without. A number of rides enter the clearing where the Warren House stands. The third on the right should be yours, leading east north-east. If you have chosen correctly, a brisk five minutes walk will bring you to a forest crossroads. The second ride on your left, leading due north, will bring you through thickets of luscious wild raspberries downhill to Pots Hole on Brockley Combe.

This is grander than Goblin Combe but spoilt by the busy road. Take it to the right for about 200 yards looking out for a steep stony track which will lead you up left through the trees. The walk has more tracks than either paths or roads at this stage. The first track right leads across a field to the elbow of a tarmac road. Follow this left uphill through a tunnel of ash and beech trees to another left turn past Home Farm. Now take the right-hand track along the top of the hill; don't get lured downhill yet unless you want to cut a mile off the walk and miss its two high spots.

A stile on the left of this track takes you down a field to the sudden, horrid edge of a quarry, such a violent assault on the limestone that you could shoot a film sequence here where the villain gets his come-uppance. The path to the right along the quarry's edge is clearly marked, stiled and visually exciting. It will lead you into a wood above Cheston Combe where you will find yourself scrambling downhill on a little sliver of the ancient Mendip forest with two huge quarry voids, more sensed than seen, one on each side of you.

At the road, cross straight over to the stile down the Church Path. St Andrews, Backwell is a must. For a start it is kept open, a rare thing these days, and has a beautiful interior screen. Its real star is its tower, where the designer has played around self-consciously with the usual Gothic mouldings, pinnacles and buttresses. Apparently it is genuine mediaeval work, but if you look carefully you will spot a repair date of 1713, so some of it at least may well be Gothick. Puzzle it out and then cut back left along the lane down past Combe Cottage, still happily ungentrified, and the little school. At the downhill bend, cross the road and take the path over the fields past Sores Court to the lane to Chelvey Farm.

This section takes some nerve as the right of way leads around and through the farm buildings. Be bold, shut the gates and carry on across the fields. Now up on your left you can see the rugged hillside and forest that you have been threading the last hour or two. When you reach Chelvey Batch lane continue through a very superior suburbia so full of neighbourhood watch signs and burglar alarms that it might make you glad you can't afford one of the houses. The last of these is the Regency thatched Brockley Cottage which is almost too picturesque and mouth-wateringly desirable.

The main road has a path and needs it. Turn left along it and endure the traffic briefly before you take the minor road right past the walled grounds of Brockley Hall. Underneath the road is a tunnel linking the gardens to the Hall which remains irritatingly hidden behind fine ironwork gates and an 1820s lodge. Just beside the lodge is a stile to the left and now a pastoral calm, unchanged since the enclosures of the 18th

Brockley Cottage

century, settles over you. Head for Brockley Court across two fields. The little church is locked but you can see its sanctus bellcote on the roof, its slim Norman doorway and read the directions in the porch to locate the so-called Pirate's Grave – a skull and crossbones with a depressing verse. The Court is a gabled 17th century gentry house whose broad window architraves had stone cross mullions before the 18th century inserted sashes.

From here to Cleeve church could be difficult but isn't because the stiles are so well kept. Three fields bring you to a lane and another stile. Three more fields follow but half way across the third, take the gate left, strike diagonally across the field and head for Cleeve's sturdily ugly neo-Norman tower. Mercifully this church is also locked but you are on the main road and it is only a step right to where you began. Perhaps the *Lord Nelson* is strategically placed!

A high walk through a forgotten Mendip demesne – Churchill, Burrington and Dolebury Warren

5.5 miles/Grade B

Maps: O.S. 1:25,000 Pathfinder ST 45/55
         O.S. 1:50,000 Landranger 172

Theme: An exciting, even sinister, territory with Victorian undertones, the high Mendips have a retired forbidding quality. This is definitely not a cosy architectural walk but a tramp through deep wood and lonely moorland marked with swallets, pots, caverns and a prehistoric city. The route is drier underfoot than you might expect, but exposed, so watch the weather.

Transport: By car – south down the A38 Taunton road as far as the big crossroads at Churchill. Park as near to this as is safe. Jews Lane, the start of the walk, actually leads off the crossroads but is far too narrow for parking (GR ST 448598).
By bus – the 820 and 821 from Bristol coach station will put you off at Churchill Gate, just before the crossroads.

Things to look out for:
1   A tremendous beech cathedral
2   A Gothick mansion smothered in forest
3   A bird's eye view of the Rock of Ages
4   Rod's Pot and Bos Swallet – gates to the underworld
5   Steep Holm when least expected
6   An empty, enigmatic city
7   Unctuous Arts and Crafts loyalty

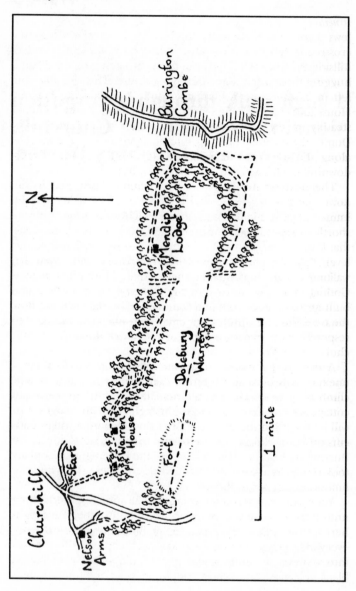

Itinerary

Jews Lane, marked, leads unobtrusively off the Churchill crossroads heading straight for the dark line of wooded hillside. As it bears left look out for a path going on uphill and hugging the garden fence of the big house. This will take you left in its time into a black fir wood. After skirting Warren House and crossing a fine two-step stile, the wider track climbs steadily up through mixed woodland for some half a mile. Don't take the next stile up into an open field but continue along the track at the forest's fringe until you hit a steep downhill track lined with superb beech trees.

The next bit needs cautious navigation. Turn steeply left down the beech avenue and take the track that leads right immediately beside the last big beech. This will bring you very shortly to a woodland crossing of ways. Take the left-hand track that leads downhill to a flat clearing. Then bear right along the level. You will find with quite a creepy shock that you are walking alongside the ivy-covered walls of Mendip Lodge – Gothick-windowed, two storeys high and very ruined. It was built around 1800 and once commanded a fine view but now the trees hide it until you are only yards away. Its owners were responsible for the smothering growth of rhododendron that chokes the wood; a haunted place.

A wide level track runs on a shelf for half a mile bursting out unexpectedly onto a neat tarmac lane. Turn right up this and climb until the surface deteriorates and a little gingerbread cottage with a white gate peeps through rampant hedges. You will be rejoining the track later, but this is where a rough path cuts off left through the fern to give dramatic views down into Burrington Combe. The cleft, where the Rev Augustus Toplady took refuge in a storm and wrote 'Rock of Ages', slices into the limestone cliff across the valley.

Your path, easy in winter, overgrown in summer, winds along until it meets a track coming up from the Combe. Turn right here and keep your eyes open for swallow holes. These are not everyone's fancy but they fascinate me. Steep paths twist down into wide round funnels and there, suddenly at your feet, a black hole gapes with water dripping down. Sometimes there is a little door with a warning notice urging you to ring 999; sometimes there is just a crack in the bracken and rocks wide enough to squeeze through. As you near the edge of the woods, Bos Swallet ('Unstable' it says) is on the left, Rod's Pot and several smaller swallow holes are on the right. Usually one or two parked cars remind you that there are pot holers creeping around underneath you.

Turn left at the wood's edge and you are back on the trail which you left earlier. Then comes a magical moment. Just as you think you are totally inland with wild moorland and gloomy forest all around, Steep Holm, islanded in the Bristol Channel, rises up in front of you like a vision set in a small triangle of muddy sea. Its not visible for long but I always look out for it.

Down to the left, but visitable, is Read's Cavern. This is another of those Mendip gateways to the underworld and it has the post holes of a prehistoric shelter cut into the low cliff above it. As you rejoin the track, a way comes in from the Forestry Commission's dreary woodlands on the left and another track climbs up to the right. Take this for a few yards and there on the left is a stile to the open downlands of the National Trust's Dolebury Warren and a complete change in landscape mood.

Climb up through the sheep to a gate and then take care not to get involved in woods again but keep to the crest of the hill with the double ditches of Dolebury rising ahead of you. As you approach them Steep Holm pops up again in the V of the gap like a rifle sight, but you forget it a minute later in the extraordinary enclosure you have entered.

Dolebury is Britain's Zimbabwe, a great stone city of tumbled anonymous Iron Age walls. It is not a flat cattle enclosure like Maes Knoll or Cadbury Castle. You are standing at the high point of a rectangular area much larger – 500 yards by 250 yards – than most mediaeval walled towns and dropping steeply down to a western entrance. Because the walls are stone and still anything from 20 to 40 feet high I find it far more memorable than the earth and grass of Maiden Castle outside Dorchester. Make a circuit of it enjoying the views and the absence of tourist hype, then drop down through the woods at

Jubilee oak, Churchill

the lower end of the walls to nondescript cottages and the main road. It should be your first car noise after five miles of wind and silence.

Immediately across the road a path leads up through the woods to a lane of very 1930s development. Down this are two pubs – the *Crown Inn*, unpretentiously rural, and the *Nelson Arms*, brick and bolder – both well placed at the end of the walk. You may be ready for home by this time, but Churchill village has a distinct and enjoyable 'Methody' character with a Methodist school room and chapel complex of 1879. Outside the *Nelson Arms* is a weedy oak tree planted in 1897 within an Arts and Crafts style enclosure far too grand for its stricken branches. Just across the road is a sturdy clocktower with a touch of the same Arts and Crafts feeling. Both oak tree and tower celebrate 'the Jubilee of her Gracious Majesty'. There is something especially Bristolian about this combination of nonconformity and demonstrative loyalty expressed in a Gothic gone plasticene and sinuous.

Walk 10

A walk in the shadow of the Wills dynasty – Blagdon, Rickford, Burrington and the high Ham

5 miles/Grade B

Maps: O.S. 1:25,000 Pathfinder ST 45/55
          O.S. 1:50,000 Landranger 172

Theme: 'Shadow' was perhaps the wrong word to use because an Edwardian high-noon lingers cheerfully on these easy hills and colour-washed villages. This walk is best described as a jolly tramp with something of everything: lofty moorland, Avon's lakeland, notable pubs, water flamboyantly on the move, all easily compassed in an afternoon.

Transport: By car – the A38 Taunton road out of Bristol; ten miles out take the left turn signed Burrington. This cuts across to the A368 where you turn left for Blagdon. In the village turn left for the free carpark. It is not a village for casual parking (GR ST 501591).
By bus – 673, 674 and 675 from Bristol coach station provide a thin service.

Things to look out for:
1	A real well with hood, bucket and chain
2	Sir George Oatley's last effort for the Wills family
3	A gauge house
4	A Freemason's lodge on a pond
5	A rood stair turret that doesn't quite make sense
6	A very surprising pit
7	Grey-green Edwardian light

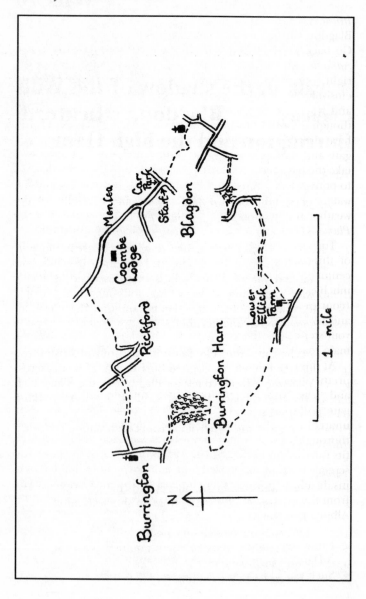

Itinerary

Blagdon village rarely runs to pavements so get out of it fast. Go back the way you came in on the A368, past the *Queen Adelaide* pub and take the Menlea, the first lane down to the right, out of the dangerous traffic. Combe Lodge rises up elusively but eminently country gentlemanlike behind walls and trees. Sir George Oatley conceived this as late as 1932 though it looks 1902. If you are trying to get glimpses of it you have already missed the well on your right. Follow the lane to a gate and stile on the left, just after a pollarded ash tree, and take the path across three fields to a lane and the steep descent to pony-ridden, water-loud Rickford. This is where the hidden waters of Mendip burst out of a green but dry valley. If the weather has been wet the hamlet will be spectacular, but the *Plume of Feathers* is textured and agreeable in rain or shine.

Turn left towards the main road so that you take in the sights of this waterworks settlement. The Gauge House, late 19th century Swiss chalet style, controls the sluices; the Mill House is much earlier, 17th–19th century, and up above it, once a chapel (courtesy of the Wills family of course), is the Masonic Lodge and its brimming reservoir. Avoid the main road by retracing your steps along the stream to the ford. Then you can cross the main road directly into Burrington Lane and Burrington.

At this point, neurotic suburbia seems to settle on a casually pretty village. There are planted specimen trees, 'no cycling' and 'leash your dog' notices, also a wholly artificial kissing gate. All the cottages, never very great shakes in these unarchitectural Mendips, have been tarted up. The place is thoroughly alive but not in any rural way. Holy Trinity Church fits Burrington perfectly. The 1913 woodwork of the pews and screens has a prim, pickled look and only a little hooded man inside and a curiously over-emphasised spirelet outside survive from the mediaeval rood screen. If you get inside look out for Albinia Jackson:

Fair, young, and happy, loving and belov'd
A Daughter cherish'd and a Wife approv'd
Such was ALBINIA; Where could life display

A fairer promise of a prosp'rous day?
Ah treacherous calm! the Sky was soon o'ercast,
Loud was the surge and direful was the blast...

Then find out what happened to her in 1810.

Up the hill now and bear left at the top, past the cherished pink and white hyped cottages until you come to woodland and can turn steeply up right between dense bushes. Moorland paths can be confusing but if you climb until you hit a distinct cross trail and turn right up it to a big outcrop of rock you are on the Burrington Ham. Sharp left at the rocks, then climb gently alongside a series of small pits. Don't be deceived by the large number of walkers; they have only staggered out of their cars a quarter of a mile away in the carpark to which the moorland trails lead down. Turn left along the road and almost immediately take the left-hand farm drive towards Lower Ellick Farm. Just before the farmyard go through the gate on the right. Ignore the tempting stile which only leads to a weedy back garden. Make instead for the gate on the skyline and cross the next field heading for a lone tree and a stile. At this point the Blagdon and Chew lakes are beginning to show. The stile drops you onto a right-leading track which turns very soon into Luvers Lane, Blagdon's spelling, not mine, and eventually into the road.

You are nearly in Blagdon but the walk is far from over as it is a strangely widespread village that runs to two estate agents, three or four pubs, a formidable rugby team and a surprise. This last is about to be sprung. Turn left down the hill, pass Westerly on your left and then take the tempting little path down to the right between bushes. Ferns, flowers and beautifully weathered rocks take your eye and then suddenly there is a great green pit on your right, a void more than 100 feet deep, full of trees and getting deeper. It is the quarry from which all this cherry coloured limestone for the cottages originally came.

At Rock Cottage and the lane, turn right and wind up to a severe notice that directs you to a path and another natural rock garden. The straight downhill lane that this path leads into has two of Blagdon's rare unravaged cottages – Tansy Cottage

Wellhead, Blagdon

and The Sheiling – their names tell you a lot about Blagdon.

Now the wonderfully arrogant 15th century church tower will be beckoning. Make for it past over-restored houses; Hannah More's house was 17th century once and a school room for an 18th century Bristol blue-stocking. The interior of the church is Blagdon's real aesthetic experience. Lord Winterstoke (Wills) got his Wills relative to rebuild it and W.D. Caroe to furnish it. Everything is just pure World War One, full of an aqueous green light with fastidiously detailed screens and pews and the glass a connected cycle, Old Testament to the left, New to the right. It is all dim, English and very memorable in a sad way; one of Avon's best churches.

A tarmac path leads out of the churchyard and swings around a deep hollow into the other half of the village where you left your car or where you can while away the hours in a pub hoping for a bus. Read the bus notices carefully.

A Grandstand walk round Dundry Hill

5.25 miles/Grade B

Maps: O.S. 1:25,000 Pathfinder ST 46/56
O.S. 1:50,000 Landranger 172

Theme: This is an easy, exhilarating, fair-weather walk with a modicum of architecture but a prodigy of views. Anyone who lives in Bristol knows the silhouette of Dundry Hill with its church, visible from almost everywhere in the city. This is a route to explore the other side of that familiar shape with surprisingly deep rural country on the very edge of creeping suburbia.

Transport: By car – south out of Bristol on the supposedly Roman road through Bishopsworth and Withywood. At the top of Broadoak Hill turn right into the village and follow the parking signs near the church to a parking place at the start of the walk (GR ST 557669).
By bus – so near, so visible, yet so far no buses to Dundry. However, a No. 75 double-decker from the Centre will take you to the foot of Broadoak Hill. This will give you a breathless beginning but a straight shortcut across the fields on the right as the housing estate ends.

Things to look out for:
1   A grim memorial to dead quarrymen
2   A stately gate in the muck of a farmyard
3   Half Somerset at your feet
4   A Celtic cattle pound
5   A Turkey factory
6   A walk on other people's rooftops (well, very nearly!)

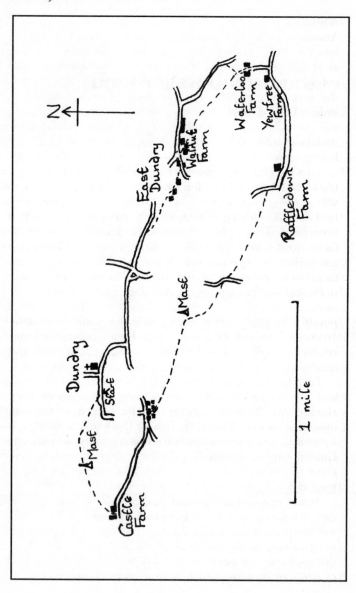

Itinerary

Assuming you arrived in a car it is worth walking the step back into the village to enjoy the churchyard. The tower is as good as St Stephen's down in the Centre – a very Gloucester-type coronet, not a Somerset tower – and most dramatic up here in the wind. The churchyard preaching cross is fine but the sinister block of plain stone hewn from the local quarry is what will remain in the mind. The village cottages are understandably rather bleak and long-suffering and some new houses cower down in the actual quarry pit to escape the blast.

Take the gate leading off the carpark and follow the rough track (beware cattle!) to the second mast. A monolithic stone stile in the corner of the field leads you to a long green slope to Castle Farm. Treat this section carefully as it is very rewarding. The right of way leads actually through the farmyard. Up above you rise two very grand late-17th century gatepiers, amazingly Carolean-baroque in such a place. But the farm buildings are equally grand, not as gabled as the great six in Pucklechurch, but with the same high relieving arches and a most unusual castellated porch. The range to the right of the porch is older than the block that faces uphill, respectively 1640 and 1670 at a guess, but the castle-style top could be 18th century. Why should a hill farm be so stately? Obviously from quarry wealth rather than sheep.

Turn left up the other side of the farm taking in the ovolo- and edge-moulded windows. Up here in the severe micro-climate the stone walls are rich in polypody ferns and mountain flowers. The next farm on the left is contemporary with Castle Farm but less ambitious. The quarry pits that made Dundry grow up on this unlikely site lie over on the left. As you come to the little estate of modern houses take the diagonal track through the middle of it to the right.

An enormous sheep pasture field is the next stage with vast, distracting views over Chew Lake and the Mendips. Keep to the top hedge all the way past the TV mast and find a gap in the hedge at the end of the field. The real path has been blocked at this stage but I am working on it. Keep left along the top hedge of three fields to the road by two modern houses. Your way continues just right of you across the road and through the gate.

Now the view is like something in a Claude Lorrain painting with Pensford viaduct looking exactly like romantic aqueducts in the Roman *campagna*. Four more fields, always along the left-hand hedge, and you are at the lane turning right to Rattledown Farm. This is unexpected, like a Regency vicarage – a B&B place, big and bold with 16-pane sash windows and a rather sly dog. Across the deep valley Maes Knoll fort tops the hill. Maes is Welsh for field and makes the point that these Iron Age camps were only cattle pounds in an age when robbers went for cattle not video recorders.

Again the view changes, this time in scale, growing more intimate and cosily rustic as you drop steeply down the lane to Yewtree Farm, white-painted and homely. Turn left here to another farm sheltered in the valley bottom. I was trying to work out a date for its cambered but clumsy windows, debating, surely not 1720, more like 1820. Then I looked at my map – Waterloo Farm! and all was settled – just post-1815 as I'd thought. Straight on through the farmyard, the track closes in with mint and mud underfoot and trees arching overhead – a real lane of pre-enclosure time with a little stone footbridge.

Abruptly this ends in a large field frivolous with heifers. It is remarkable how motherhood sobers down a cow. If you climb up the lane you will have to pass close to those long, aluminium sheds that lie uneasily up the hill. They have a certain horrid fascination with a warm breath of myriad turkeys blowing from their wire netting, white feathers caught in all the hedges and sudden bursts of companionable gobbling. More sensitive souls should take the path to the left along the length of this field, safely below the turkey sheds, and reach the lane through the buildings of 1820ish Walnut Farm. That particular decade saw much activity in this valley – land values rising with the war perhaps.

Now comes a delightful section of the walk that requires a little courage as the right of way seems to run through a number of people's back gardens. This is East Dundry, a very choice village where the most intelligent commuters in Bristol have settled in seclusion so private that I hesitate to describe the route.

Dundry church tower

Turn left down Spring Lane. Cross Cottage above you on the right has a difficult datestone that I interpret as 1819 but could be a hundred years out. Edge-moulded mullion and a dripstone to your left, but take the path leading gently uphill to your right, well before Spring Farm. Now follows an enchanting sequence when you are almost walking on the roofs of a series of highly desirable old houses tucked beneath you on the steep hillside, the last of them the best – 17th century and postcard-pretty.

The track downhill is not for you. After this last house mount the almost precipitous down, pass two ash trees and a gap in the hedge to reach the lane. Now, at last, all Bristol lies before you, looking dreadful, which is why I have kept from this side of Dundry until now. Bus walkers will turn right down Broadoak Hill. Car walkers should cross the road along Crabtree Lane to return to ever-bracing Dundry and the carpark. A walk like wine if the weather is right.

Abandoned mines and a pre-historic Canterbury – Pensford and Stanton Drew

Just over 7 miles/Grade A

Maps: O.S. 1:25,000 Pathfinder ST 66/76 & ST 46/56
O.S. 1:50,000 Landranger 172

Theme: So richly textured that it is hard to characterise, but those who never walk this north Mendip/Bristol sub-land will never know their Bristol. Deeply-scored prehistoric tracks and stone circles prove its age, 17th century farms tell of early prosperity, then came coal mines and industry. All are submerged now in a gentle country of well-watered fields and mild hills.

Transport: By car – park in Pensford village about 6 miles out of Bristol on the A37 Wells road (GR ST 618638).
By bus – there is an hourly service out to Pensford on the 376 from Bristol coach station. Get off in the village at the bottom of the hill.

Things to look out for:
1   That viaduct – why travel to see the Pont du Gard?
2   An old mill by the stream
3   A Bronze Age cathedral that neither hippies nor tourists have wrecked
4   A contrast in farmhouse restorations
5   Where Bristol's water runs pure
6   The ghost of a lost tramway
7   Slag from the original Bristol blue glass factory
8   A colliers' path through a new jungle

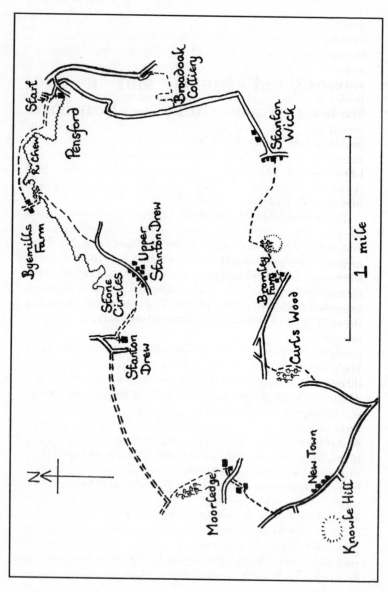

Itinerary

Pensford (birthplace of Acker Bilk!) is a most rewarding village though it might be wise to keep the exploration for your return since the pleasures include both a pub, the *Rising Sun*, and a restaurant. One ashlar-faced cottage is actually built on a bridge and the church is penned in between running streams. The miners' institute and a large Victorian school record how recently an industry has died here and a domed stone lock-up just across the main road suggests what a tough little place it was in its heyday. Two astonishing flood markers show what the Chew can get up to and, of course, there is the tremendous viaduct striding over the place carrying nothing to nowhere now the Radstock line is closed.

Take the little lane that leads off north of the river just above the pub. It turns into a green track under the viaduct's arches and almost immediately the typical, rich flora of coal-bearing measures surrounds you. A stile and three fields along the river will bring you out at Byemills Farm, a handsome relaxed 18th century house on the track down to the mill. Only the weirs keep the Chew deep enough to please the many anglers. Cross the river and take the stile on the right for another four fields bringing you out by a little Gothic-arched mediaeval footbridge on a narrow lane leading into Upper Stanton Drew. High up on the bank on the left is a splendid, though dilapidated, long pantiled roof, then rather too much infilling. A stile and path off the raised footway on the right will bring you through three fields to a point where you can overlook all three of Stanton Drew's stone circles. John Wood, the architect who planned 18th century Bath, was an antiquary in his spare time and fascinated by the stones. He laid out the King's Circus in Bath with the same diameter as the best preserved circle here at Stanton Drew – the one he called the Moon Circle which you can see down the field to your right. His Sun Circle is in the field to the left above the heap of tyres.

These are some of the most relaxed and satisfying prehistoric remains in Britain: great chunks of smooth red rock lying in the hayfields. The mediaeval Church Farm with its unrestored Decorated window is equally interesting. Not so the locked church but you can spy the weird twisted stones of The Cove over the churchyard wall. Go down into the village, left at the oddly-angled house, then right at the village hall before the *Druids Arms*. This track begins with endearingly inappropriate suburban villas then plunges down between cliff-like banks to reveal itself as the old way in from the west to the sacred stone circles.

As this track bends to the right, go through a gate to the left. The path takes you over five fields along an informal nature reserve, a strange marshy tract of nut bushes. Then comes the first of the two Moorledge houses. This late 17th century farm in warm brown stone has been determinedly transformed into a small gentry house. Across the road a farm track leads to the second Moorledge, equally old, equally deserving, but preserving its 19th century casement windows and a fine ogee-headed datestone – 1665. The path leads between the farm buildings through into the rickyard where you can see the stile on the right leading into a hill field which you must climb to reach the lane.

Turn left here. Knowle Hill, an old mining area, is prominent to the south and the lane leads through New Town, once miners' houses, to Gold's Cross and the purifying beds for Chew Valley Lake. A steep lane downhill to the left takes you over a tiny stream to a stile right and a pleasant three field path, keeping Curls Wood, another lost mine, on your left. At the lane, keep right, heading for the curious pyramid, first forested then deforested, of Bromley pit bank. At Bromley Farm prepare for trouble, but only cowards stick always to the roads!

The right of way goes off left between the farm buildings – inevitably there is a dog – but make downhill for the pit bank and step into its lower, still jungled, slopes. The path leads down to a wooden bridge on the left, before the end of the wood, back into the fields. Within living memory all this was soot and steam. Follow the hedge down but take the first path right. Avon have make an excellent job of the stiles, but Avonfolk have not supported them by treading the paths. Half way up the next field you will be crossing the tramway that linked, quite recently, Bromley pit to Broadoak colliery and the Radstock line. Up two

Standing stone, Stanton Drew

more fields guided by the stiles and you will be standing by a line of cottages which is all that survives of the factory that produced the famous Bristol blue glass in the late 17th and 18th centuries. The first cottage has lumps of the iridescent slag lying on its wall. Leave them there.

Turn left then right at the lane, pass the *Carpenters Arms* in Stanton Wick and you will come to Broadoak colliery. The last manager here refused to be rescued from a fall until the pit ponies were rescued first. I know because his daughter, an old lady now, told me all about it. Here a mini industrial estate threatens you with open pools of dangerous chemicals. You can simply follow the lane down to Pensford with lost industry at every turning. Only if you are still feeling energetic and the nettles are not grown high, take the right of way leading off right into the old colliery yard through the second gate by the threatening notices. This route twists excitingly round down the spoil heap of scrubby oak growth, over concrete miners' stiles of the 1930s to the overgrown rail track which has orchids and much atmosphere. The path leads you down, then over a field to a track across the stream and so up to the busy main road and back to Pensford; thus concluding a 3000 year historical circuit.

The valley between the tunnels and the last relics of the ancient forest of Kingswood

3.5 miles/Grade C, but an extra half mile if you go by bus

Maps: O.S. 1:25,000 Pathfinder ST 66/76 & ST 67/77
O.S. 1:50,000 Landranger 172

Theme: An exploration of that remote wooded valley you glimpse briefly between tunnels soon after the train leaves Temple Meads for Bath. A short towpath walk on Bristol's doorstep where the Avon still lingers under lily pads and the last scraps of a Norman hunting forest are taking over again.

Transport: By car – take the A431 out of Bristol through St George. Two-and-a-half miles out at a small roundabout turn right for Hanham Green. Soon after the houses end fork right for Hanham Mills at a tall grove of lime trees; this is Tillies Green. Park in the gravelled lay-by on the right (GR ST 648704). By bus – nothing quite goes to Tillies Green, so take one of the frequent 44/45s from Old Market and get off at Hanham Common. Walk straight on a few hundred yards and take the first turning on the right down Castle Farm Road. Immediately after the farm the lane forks left, becomes Riverside, and the walking circuit comes in on your left.

Things to look out for:
1   Bristol's Thelwell country – a paradise for young riders
2   Kipling's recipe for the mystic woods of Albion
3   Brunel's engineering from an odd angle
4   All that remains of a mill for splitting iron and rolling lead
5   An 18th century towpath bridge
6   Parish marker SW4
7   Sally on the Barn – a folly face

83

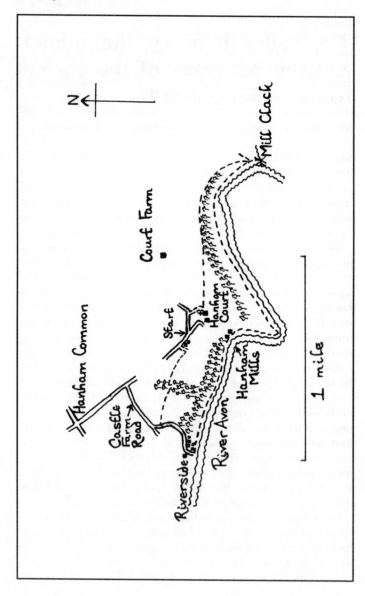

Itinerary

Car travellers will start at Tillies Green. Go back a few yards towards Bristol until you come to a tree-shadowed pond. Turn left just before it and cross a double stile in the lee of Old Oak House. Far across the fields you will see Brislington House but keep close to the hedge on your right that separates you from a field hyperactive with ponies. Quite suddenly after crossing a stile you are in a fragment of Kingswood. Bristol was originally a mere part of the royal manor of that vast forest, but coal and iron ore lay just 50 feet down and the colliers working in no less than 72 small pits soon made short work of the deer. There is a quarry immediately on your left as you go down the stream. Cross by the iron bridge, not the concrete one, and you are back in the field again coming to Riverside Lane where bus travellers join the walk.

The lane pitches downhill to the left. Here over the old quarries the forest is regenerating sturdily with oak, ash and thorn predominant like the Wealden Forest which features in Kipling's *Puck of Pook's Hill.* Over the next mile or so you get the feeling of how quickly the forest would take our whole island back if we ever left it. But now you are down into that intriguingly isolated group of cottages that you must have noticed if you have taken a train from Bristol to Bath.

Rather unimaginatively they are known as Riverside and in the last few years gentrification has lain heavily on them with bow windows, bottle glass, strap-pointing and unsuitable hardwood casements. The only cottage that looks as they all used to look is No. 15, but no one has spoilt the river yet. It flows slow, deep and brown but not dirty, made navigable by a series of widely spaced weirs and locks in 1723. Before that the many industrial mills along its course had blocked navigation, though back in Richard Coeur de Lion's reign it was possible to travel by wine boat all the way up to Bath.

Turn left along the towpath (often muddy in winter) and you will pass some rather sad small fields that must once have made the Riverside cottagers virtually self-supporting. Now an army of nettle and thistle has taken them over, the fate of such peasant smallholdings all over Europe. The 17th century

Baptists used to meet here for worship and escape the magistrates by nipping over the river into Somerset. What makes this deep wooded valley so bizarre is the frequent sudden thunder of trains bursting in and out of tunnels across the river. Here, on these last stages of his broad gauge to Bristol, Brunel built deliberately educational tunnel entrances in the styles of mediaeval architecture. The last one before Temple Meads was Norman, but that got lost when they turned the tunnel into a cutting.

The more mellow roar of the weir at the locks tells you that you have reached the limits of the Bristol Port Authority. This is Hanham Mills, a very old industrial settlement. The gaunt mill owner's house has the date 1726, but they were rolling iron and lead here and splitting steel much earlier. The idyllic wooded scene is a recent development. In 1695 a station was set up here on the river to take water to Bristol in elmwood pipes. There was another pumping station at Crews Hole and a reservoir at Lawrence Hill.

Beware of some spiteful dogs here. I always take a stout stick for self-defence on any walk as country dogs usually behave like characters in a horror movie. The two pubs are *The Old Lock & Weir* and *The Chequers*; the latter is really a restaurant and there is also a childrens' playground. On summer evenings it is all very Bristolian bucolic, often with live bands playing – a revival of the Edwardian pleasure garden but reached by car now, not by boat. Surprisingly few craft use the river.

Press on along the towpath into a completely different world of wide meadows, willow trees and a distant sweep to the palatial chocolate factory at Keynsham. If you want to know what a portico with columns in antis looks like, then one is staring you in the face. Sweet manufacturers always tended to architectural gestures – Fry's trying to outdo Cadbury's at Bournville. On your left is a fine crescent of rising woodlands. You can find Chaucer's 'Gaitres' or dogwood berried here in the autumn, they are an odd lipstick pink with scarlet seeds. Even the grand river meadow, Eden's Field, which you are crossing seems to be reverting to nettle and thistle, but it must be almost inaccessible from any farm. If you are walking in summer you will find the Avon as flowery as the fields, covered with yellow water lilies.

A fourth field, Cleves, brings you to the end of the wood and a scene straight out of Constable. The path is signed left up to Willsbridge, but it is worth going on a few yards over the bridge across Mill Clack Brook and down the steps to the Avon to enjoy the scene. The water is quite tropically overcrowded with literally thousands of fish, some quite large and edible, all milling about in the shallows. The bridge is a perfect survival of the early 18th century canalization and even the little Mill Clack seems to have had a quay. The isolated cottage is neat limestone and pantiles to the front, but wholly hit-and-miss to the rear.

Mill Clack Bridge

Back to the stile and follow the path up, keeping close to the edge of the wood. This is the old Common Field of mediaeval Hanham but the modern crop is golf balls because someone with an erratic drive uses the field to practise. Between Mill Clack bridge and Hanham Church there is a parish marker stone with SW4 carved on its face. See if you can spot it; you don't have to leave the path.

The long, steady climb is rewarded with a handsome stone stile and a rather sinister view of the Bristol suburbs reaching out greedily to snatch farmland. Over on the right is Court Farm with its well-known folly, Sally-on-the-Barn. There is a stone statue of the goddess Ceres perched on the barn roof and the windows have been placed to suggest a face. There is an unlikely legend about it being a memorial to a singing girl; 1810 would be a likely date for this kind of architectural trick. To the left, down in the trees, is all that can be seen of Hanham Court but go downhill through the kissing gate, made in the old Avonmouth Ironworks, and a narrow path will bring you out in the churchyard at the side of this carefully screened Court.

The spired gazebo-tower that you will have spotted from the hill is 19th century and the picturesque huddle next to the church is mainly 16th century, the building of a rich Bristol clothier called John Lacey. The hidden face of the house is 18th century, an addition made by the Cresswicks who bought the Court in 1638 and hung on for two centuries. They entertained James II here by killing and roasting the last stag of Kingswood Forest, a very non-environmental gesture. This was intended to soothe the Catholic monarch after a force of local nonconformist miners had joined the Duke of Monmouth's rebellious army when it was camped at Keynsham.

St George's has Norman interior details behind its dull Victorian Gothic exterior but you are unlikely to see them as it is resolutely locked up. The 15th century barn is the last relic of a grange belonging to Keynsham Abbey. Take the church drive down to the road, turn left and you will find yourself back in Tillies Green. Bus travellers should finish the circuit by turning back to the first part of this description but car owners are home and dry.

Glossary

Ashlar Masonry walling made of large, smooth, even blocks.

Bulls-eye Window A small, circular or elliptical window.

Cambered Arch An arch with a gradual, shallow curve.

Columns in Antis Columns between two antae, that is pilasters of which the base and capital do not conform with the order used elsewhere on the building.

Commonwealth Period of building from c.1640 to 1660.

Cottage Orné A small house, usually thatched, with decorative architectural trimmings such as leaded lights and carved wooded verandahs.

Double-pile House An English 17th century type: a rectangular block two rooms deep, the two rows of rooms usually being separated by a corridor running the length of the house.

Dripstone A stone moulding projecting over and round the heads of windows and doorways in order to throw off rainwater.

Gazebo A small look-out tower or summerhouse with a view.

Gothick Unscholarly 18th century revival of pointed-arch Gothic.

Infill	Modern buildings within an area of older buildings.
Loggia	A gallery, or separate structure, open on one or more sides, sometimes pillared.
Misericord	A bracket on the underside of the seat of a hinged choir stall which, when turned up, served as a support for the occupant while standing during long services.
Mounting Block	A series of blocks of stone to enable riders to mount and dismount from horses.
Mullion	A vertical strip, usually of masonry, dividing a window into two or more lights: a) Chamfered: a rectangular mullion with its edges cut off diagonally. b) Cross: two intersecting mullions dividing a window into four lights. c) Edge-moulded: a rectangular mullion whose face has incised lines. d) Ovolo-moulded: a rectangular mullion whose outer face projects forward in an oval curve.
Ogee	A double-curved line made up of a convex and concave part (S or inverted S).
Pantile	A clay roofing tile of curved section resembling a flattened S.
Pargetting	Exterior plastering of a timber-framed building.
Pennant	Fine-grained Coal Measures sandstone formerly quarried in the north-east suburbs of Bristol.

Root House	Ornamental building in a landscape often constructed from the roots or bark of trees.
Sanctus Bellcote	Framework housing a bell, placed directly over the chancel arch. This enabled the bell to be rung three times at the points of consecration in the mass so that farmworkers in the fields could cross themselves at the right time even though they could not attend the service.
Scraped	Drastically restored, usually in the 19th century, removing all original features.
Scrollwork	Curvaceous, decorative features in the form of a scroll.
Strap-pointing	Mortar joints in brick or stone work which stand proud of the masonry.
Stucco	Plasterwork usually rendered very smooth or modelled as in stucco ceilings.

Country Code

Guard against all risk of fire
Every year costly damage is done by fire to crops, plantations, woodlands and heaths. Picnic fires not properly put out are one cause. A cigarette thrown away or a pipe knocked out can start a raging inferno. Be careful – a spark may do terrible damage and destroy a lifetime's work.

Fasten all gates
Animals, if they stray, can do great damage to crops and to themselves. Wandering animals are a menace to themselves and others on country roads. Even if you find a gate open, always shut it behind you.

Keep your dogs under close control
It is natural for a dog to chase anything that will run. Keep your dog out of temptation's way. Animals are easily frightened and the chasing of a ewe or cow may result in loss of young. When near animals or walking along the road, keep your dog on a lead.

Keep to public paths across farmland
Crops are damaged by treading, at any stage of growth. Patches of flattened corn make it difficult to harvest. Grass is also a valuable crop, remember. So please walk in single file where a path crosses a field. This keeps the path well defined and saves the crops on either side.

Use gates and stiles to cross fences, hedges and walls
If you force your way through a fence or hedge, you will weaken it. Where a person has gone an animal may follow. Stones dislodged from walls may injure people and animals, and damage crops and machinery.

Take your litter home

All litter is unsightly. Broken glass, tins and plastic bags are dangerous. They may also damage costly machinery and hold up work which it is vital to finish while the weather lasts. So leave no litter or picnic remains.

Help to keep all water clean

Water is precious in the country. Never wash dishes or bathe in somebody's water supply or foul it in any other way, or interfere with water-troughs set for cattle.

Protect wildlife, plants and trees

Wild flowers give more pleasure to more people if left to grow. Plants should never be uprooted. Trees are valuable as well as beautiful: if they are damaged their health and beauty is harmed. Birds and their eggs, animals, plants and trees should be left alone.

Take special care on country roads

Drive carefully. Blind corners, hump-backed bridges, slow-moving farm machinery and led or driven animals are all hazards for the motorist. Walk carefully too. It is generally safer to walk on the right, facing oncoming traffic.

Respect the life of the countryside

The life of the countryside centres on its work. While you are there, try to fit in. Country people have to leave their belongings in the open, roads and paths run through their places of work, and you are on trust. Their work often involves hard labour. They keep early hours. So make as little noise as possible when you pass through villages in the evening. Be considerate, leave things alone, and so repay the local people for the pleasure their countryside has given you.